THE LITTLE BOOK OF
PEACE OF MIND

THE LITTLE BOOK OF
PEACE OF MIND

SUSAN JEFFERS, Ph.D.

Jeffers
press

THE LITTLE BOOK OF PEACE OF MIND

Published by Jeffers Press, a division of Susan Jeffers, LLC

P.O. Box 5338, Santa Monica, California 90049-5338, USA

First published as *The Little Book of Peace* in Great Britain in
2001 by Hodder and Stoughton, a division of
Hodder Headline, and in Australia and New Zealand by
Hodder Headline Australia Pty Limited

www.susanjeffers.com

Library of Congress Control Number: 2004107100

ISBN: 0-9745776-5-0

Cover design by Dotti Albertine

Manufactured in China

First Jeffers Press edition 2004

do the work
let go of the fight
embrace the flow
aah, peace...
SJ

CONTENTS

INTRODUCTION

ALL IS WELL!

Peace of mind...where does it come from? It is clear to me that those who approach life with serenity rather than struggle have discovered the secret of "dancing with life." They have learned how to move into the flow of their experiences—good or bad—with a feeling of harmony, trust, gratitude, and love. They have found a way of convincing their frightened minds that "ALL IS WELL." The good news is that we can all learn how to dance with life as well.

Throughout this little book, you will find in capsule form many of the calming thoughts found in *End the Struggle and Dance with Life.* I encourage you to read it over and over and over again. And when the weight of the world seems to be getting you down, open it to any page to help lighten your spirits. In time, the healing messages within will teach you the real meaning of a peaceful mind.

I've come a long way on this issue of creating a peaceful mind and

I'm amazed at how obvious are
the causes of our upsets in life,
big or small. I'm reminded of the
ancient saying, "The road is
smooth. Why do you throw rocks
before you?" We all throw rocks
before us, sometimes making
our Journey very difficult. So
let's begin clearing the debris to
make way for a more joyful,
abundant... and peaceful... life!

From My Heart to Yours...

Susan Jeffers

RISING ABOVE

THE CLOUDS

SOMETHING WONDROUS IN YOUR BEING

I have a wonderful statue of the Laughing Buddha. He is always there to remind me that true joy comes not from something out there, but from something wondrous within our being. This "something wondrous" is ever-present and always accessible. As a result, we all have the ability to reach this place within where we can feel safe, abundant and truly able to dance with life.

IT'S THERE
FOR THE TAKING

I call the wondrous place within
our being the Higher Self. When
we "live" in the realm of the
Higher Self, we experience
all the divine qualities such as
caring, joy, strength, appreciation,
and love. We are free to enjoy the
best that life has to offer. Peace
and laughter fill our hearts.

"HIGHER"
IS BETTER!

The Higher Self is the Spiritual part of who we are. Most of us live in the Lower Self. This is the place of struggle, lack, fear, and pain. The good news is that we can begin the Journey toward that place of inner peace right now, right where we are, and with the tools that are presently in our grasp.

THERE IS POWER IN THE HIGHER SELF

The Higher Self knows we have the strength to handle anything that can ever happen to us. It doesn't see the outside world as a threat; it sees it as a place to learn and grow and contribute. The Higher Self knows that all situations in our life—good or bad—can be used as a teaching for our highest good.

TUNE IN TO THE WISDOM WITHIN

Our Higher Self holds wisdom beyond our wildest dreams. This incredible wisdom can lead us to exactly where we need to go for our highest good. If we listen, this is what we hear:

"It's all happening perfectly.
Whatever happens in my life,
I'll handle it. I'll learn from it.
I'll make it a triumph!"

THE WORLD IS HUGE WITH POSSIBILITY!

When the Journey inward
to the Higher Self begins,
life expands to encompass a world
that is HUGE with possibility.
Bringing a Spiritual dimension
into all that we do is essential for
ending the struggle and dancing with
life. Our bodies and our minds
can take us only so far. Our Spirit
can lead us all the way home.

THE HIGHER SELF IS THE KEY TO FREEDOM

If you never rise above the level of the Lower Self, you will never feel free. If you transcend to the Higher Self, you will always feel free— despite what is happening in the outside world! Your inner peace has nothing to do with the dramas of your life. (What a relief!) When you find your way to your Higher Self, the Laughing Buddha inside of you will truly begin to laugh!

RELEASE

LETTING GO OF HOLDING ON

Most of us don't know how to let go. In fact, we wear life like a girdle—tight, hard, rigid, uncomfortable, and constricting. Oh, how we long to take off that girdle and breathe deeply and freely! Oh, how we long to let go of all those things that keep us immersed in struggle. We long to fly above the clouds! Yes, it's definitely time to let go!

IT FEELS GOOD TO LOOSEN UP

I love the image of "wearing the world as a loose garment." This means: 1) not hanging on so tightly to the way it's supposed to be; 2) trusting that all is well... that life is happening perfectly; 3) seeing the possibility of love and growth that exists in all experiences—good and bad; 4) recognizing that we can face the ebb and flow of life from a place of harmony and peace instead of struggle.

DANCING WITH LIFE

How can we ever learn to dance
with life when we are uptight?
Dancing with life by definition
means curving, blending, bending,
circling and flowing—like nature.
"Bad" dancers are straight, stiff and
methodical, totally out of harmony
with the ceaseless flow of the
energy of the Universe.

GO AROUND THE OBSTACLES

We can learn a lot by watching how water relates to the world around it. It's fluid. It goes around any obstacle in its way. (It doesn't stop to argue!) It flows downstream rather than struggling to push upstream as many of us are doing in life. It just goes with the flow. Perhaps that's why watching the action and rhythm of water is so peaceful to the human psyche.

GO WITH THE FLOW

We weren't born to hold onto positions. We are meant to flow in a world that is constantly moving beneath our feet. Say to yourself:

"I am free. I am fluid. I am rich. I am whole. I embrace it all. I am nourished. I have much to give. I can soar. I am at peace. I let go."

UN-SET YOUR HEART

Setting your heart on something is
entering into a state of rigidity. Un-
setting your heart is entering a state
of flow. Create as many goals as you
want. Picture exactly what you
would like to happen. With loving
effort, do the necessary work.
And when you are satisfied that
you have done as much as you can,
LET GO OF THE OUTCOME.

IT'S ALL ALRIGHT!

Think about the many little things that cause upset in your life: Forgetting to buy something at the market. Sitting in the airport for hours because the plane was delayed. Rain when you have invited people over for a picnic. It's at these times that we really need to ask ourselves a very profound question: *WHAT IF THIS WAS ALL ALRIGHT?* Instant peace of mind!

SAYING "YES" FEELS SO GOOD

Saying YES reduces upset
and anxiety and lets you
become the creator of enriching
new life experiences. Saying
YES doesn't mean giving up.
It means getting up and acting
on your belief that you can
create meaning and purpose in
whatever life hands you.
It means moving into
the realm of action.

In the realm of action,
you are able to:

FIND THE BLESSING. FIND
THE LESSON TO BE LEARNED.
FIND THE STRENGTH YOU
NEVER THOUGHT YOU HAD.
FIND THE TRIUMPH.

Saying YES is a very
powerful tool indeed!

DECIDE TO SAY "YES"

Decide that you have the power
to say YES to it all. Your saying YES
guarantees that you will find the
limitless source of inner strength
that lies within. There is no
greater comfort than that.
When we achieve that state of
comfort, we can let go
of our need to control not only
the little things, but even the
big things in our lives.

CUT THE CORD

We can't control the behavior of others. We must let go and let people in our lives follow their own path. Co-dependency is an inability to establish healthy boundaries between ourselves and others. As a result, their behavior determines our self-esteem, happiness, and sense of peace and flow. When we cut the cord, we are free...and so are they. Hallelujah!

CREATE YOUR OWN HAPPINESS

There is no inner peace when we depend on other people to fill us up. It feels so much better when we fill ourselves up. If peace in your heart is dependent on how other people are going to act, you are living in the realm of the Lower Self and you will constantly be in conflict. As you cut the cord, you are free to live in the realm of the Higher Self where happiness reigns.

SIMPLICITY
BRINGS CALM

Anything that takes away our
lightness-in-living definitely weighs
us down. It is wise to lighten the
load—in all areas of your life. You
can't end the struggle when you
are carrying so much weight
within and around you. The trick
is to release that which weighs
you down and embrace that
which makes you soar.
Are you flying yet?

LET GO OF EXCESS BAGGAGE

Use and enjoy that which enriches your life and let the rest go. Start with cleaning your closets. "Susan, why, in the grand scope of life, is cleaning our closets so important?" Because it creates a "trickle-down" of relief: As you get rid of the clutter in your closet, you begin to realize you don't need (or want!) as much as you thought you did. What a relief!

WHAT "DON'T" YOU NEED?

When you clean your closets, you realize you don't need to buy as many things, which means...You don't need as much space, which means...You don't need to have a bigger house, which means...You don't need to earn as much, which means...You don't need to work so hard, which means...You have more time and energy, which means...PEACE AT LAST!

ENOUGH IS TRULY ENOUGH!

The word "ENOUGH" can overcome the hunger of our MORE–BETTER–BEST society. ENOUGH implies a sense of fullness. When we say "I've had enough" at the end of a delicious meal, it means we are full and satisfied. We are not looking for more. When we include thoughts of ENOUGH in the deepest recesses of our being, we can begin to relax and smell the proverbial roses.

A NEW KIND OF EXCELLENCE

Competition as we know it today is crazy-making and demoralizing. There is a wonderful alternative. We can achieve excellence by acting on our understanding that we have a higher meaning and purpose in this world in whatever form that takes. When we connect with that sense of higher meaning and purpose, our "performance" is without equal.

THERE IS
ALWAYS MORE

You never have to hold onto
anything. You can love it all,
enjoy it all, but you need not
hang on. *There is always more.*
As you let go of all the fear and
suffering that attachment brings,
you are free. Feel the relief this
freedom brings. Feel yourself
lighten as you let go of all the
unnecessary burdens you have
created for yourself.

SEEING WITH

NEW EYES

THE TIME IS "NOW"

It is time to focus on the miracle of NOW. Most of us are focused on the future. We are constantly waiting for the big moment when our goals, dreams, and desires will be fulfilled. That guarantees us a life of wishing, wanting, and lack of fulfilment. It doesn't have to be that way. We can focus on the gifts and richness of the NOW!

LET GO OF
"GETTING THERE"

Inner peace comes from knowing
we have so much right now...
family, friends, career, opportunities
for contribution and personal
growth, and more. With this
knowledge, we realize that we are
not simply machines trying to
reach a destination. We are hearts
and souls vibrantly connected to
everyone and everything around us
each moment of each day!

THE GIFT OF THE PRESENT

We are told that first we sow the seeds and later we harvest. In truth, we don't have to wait for later. When we focus on the beauty of the now, each moment can be exquisite. When we focus on the beauty of the now, we are filled with a sense of gratitude. When we focus on the beauty of the now, we are able to harvest WHILE we are sowing the seeds!

IT'S ALL A MATTER OF PERCEPTION

If you see your tasks in life as drudgery, then they are drudgery. On the other hand, if you see them as a gift of the Universe coming through you, then your tasks are done in the spirit of love and generosity. What a difference your perception makes!

CLIMB OFF THE LADDER TO DISTRESS

Success is not about goals. Success is about living a full and balanced life in partnership with others to create a joyful feeling of love, contribution, appreciation and abundance...*despite how our endeavors may turn out.*

FORGET ABOUT THE GOAL!

We can't learn the art of letting go when one eye is on the goal. Nor can we learn the art of embracing all that is beautiful when one eye is on the goal. That's just the way it is. We must keep both eyes on the enjoyment of the process and forget about the goal!

WE ARE ALL
"GOOD ENOUGH"

Human beings were not born to
be perfect. We were born to learn,
to grow, to expand, to love, to
create, to enjoy, and to see the
beauty in all things—including
ourselves. Our striving for
perfection is a futile endeavor, a
waste of time. Even the most
enlightened of us regularly trip
and fall. No one is perfect...
even the Buddhas have their days!

ENJOY!

Feelings of accomplishment and satisfaction do not come from striving to be perfect. They do come from the process of using our inner power, beauty and love in a creative, expansive, positive and loving way. It doesn't get any better than that.

IF WE LEARN AND GROW FROM OUR MISTAKES, THEN THEY AREN'T MISTAKES.

IF YOU HAVEN'T MADE ANY MISTAKES LATELY, YOU MUST BE DOING SOMETHING WRONG!

EVERYONE HAS THEIR OWN DANCE TO DANCE

Some of us want to spread our arms wide to new adventures. Some of us want to open the curtain just a little bit for the time being. Some of us want to light a huge bonfire. Some of us want just a little flame to radiate our own special light into the world. Never worry if you are doing it "wrong." There is no wrong. It's your dance. Every day it's a new dance for all of us. Trust your own rhythm. It suits you.

SAY "YES" TO SAYING "NO!"

Saying NO is not always a negative. When we say NO to tasks that overburden us and take away our peace of mind, it is a positive. In the beginning, saying NO can bring on great anxiety. That's okay! FEEL THE FEAR AND SAY NO ANYWAY! As you break the self-destructive habit of taking on more than you can comfortably handle, your body and your mind will breathe a sigh of relief!

FOLLOW YOUR HEART

Shoulds and shouldn'ts are signs of our need to conform. They come from the Lower Self. They make us worry. They make us do too much, think too much, plan too much. They make us lose sight of who we really are. Remember that from a Higher Self perspective, our enjoyment and contribution to life come from following our own heart...and everyone's heart is different.

BE YOUR OWN PERSON

Tune into the wisdom within. The Higher Self holds wisdom beyond our wildest dreams that can lead us to exactly where we need to go for our highest good. Simply ask your Higher Self what is right for you to do relative to your purpose here on earth, listen for the loving response, then act accordingly. This is being your own person. This is being the best that you can be.

BALANCE IS BEAUTIFUL

A balanced life is a gift we can give ourselves. A balanced life is one that is filled with the riches of play, intimacy with family and friends, work, alone time, and personal growth and more. When we feel abundant, our addiction to work falls by the wayside, which is where it belongs!

TAKE CHARGE OF YOUR LIFE

For peace of mind, it is essential that we learn to let go of the victim mentality. The truth is that we are not helpless and weak. All things in our lives can be used to empower us, no matter how difficult they are at the time. Instead of blaming others, we need to learn how to take charge of our lives, honor who we are, and create powerful and beautiful lives for ourselves.

SAY "NO" TO BLAME... "YES" TO PERSONAL POWER!

Any time we blame anyone or anything for what is happening in our lives, we are giving away all our power and our peace of mind. If there is a hell on earth, living as a victim with feelings of anger and blame defines it. If there is a heaven on earth, living powerfully and lovingly as the creator of our own lives defines it.

TRUST
THE UNIVERSE

It is obvious that peace cannot exist
within our hearts with the presence
of fear. I have the perfect antidote:
Whenever fear enters your being,
simply look up and say:

**"Okay, Universe. Take over,
please. Take me where you
wish. I'll enjoy the ride."**

And then find ways of
enjoying the ride. Perfect!

FIND THE GIFT
IN ALL THINGS

No matter how difficult life may seem, we can find meaning and purpose in it all. We can learn and grow from even the most challenging situations in our lives. As we learn we can handle it all in a powerful and loving way, our confidence grows and grows and grows. In that lies the gift.

THE TEARS
OF "YES"

It feels so good to enter the Land of
Tears. What a merciful relief not to
have to hold back that raging river of
emotion! The tears of "YES" remind
us that we are part of the human race.
They teach us to have compassion for
others as we remember that deep within
them exists their own Land of Tears, no
matter how they may appear on the
outside. The tears of "YES" are such
a beautiful symbol of the human spirit.

WHEN OPPOSITES GO TOGETHER

Joy and sorrow flow together, the one embracing the other. Just as we can flow in the peace of happy experiences, we can flow in the pain of unhappy experiences knowing we will always get to the other side. It helps to see it all as just part of the richness of life.

WE ARE
IN CONTROL

While we can't really ever control anything "out there," we can learn to control the most important thing...our REACTION to whatever life hands us. When we are in control of our reactions, we can be battered by the world around us and still maintain a wonderful sense of inner peace.

FIND PEACE IN THE MYSTERY

Tranquillity comes when we stop asking "WHY?" I've often been asked, "Why is there so much suffering in the world?" If this question weighs heavily on your mind, I suggest you stop driving yourself crazy by expecting an answer that we ordinary mortals can't provide. Instead, when the question comes up, tell yourself the following:

"I can't see the Grand Design,
the Divine plan for this
Universe. Therefore, I no longer
will ask why. Instead, I will learn
to be more trusting.
Life includes suffering. And
it is up to me to find a way to
be more peaceful and
compassionate in the midst
of the suffering."

WE DON'T KNOW THE "GRAND DESIGN"

When we let go of our expectations, we can allow ourselves the peaceful thought that it's all happening perfectly, no matter how it turns out. The truth is that blessings surround us all the time. We need to focus on the blessings. That shift in focus isn't a delusion. In fact: We are deluding ourselves when we focus on the bad!

WE CAN HANDLE IT ALL!

Yes, life is filled with surprises, some good and some bad. But with the inner knowing that we can handle anything life hands us, we don't have to worry about the future any longer. We can get on with our life with a feeling of freedom and adventure. We can even begin to enjoy the mysteries, instead of feeling threatened by them. It doesn't get any better than that!

FIND
YOUR CENTER

ACQUIRE "SEA LEGS"

Acquiring sea legs is about letting
go of our resistance and going
with the movement below our
feet. In so doing we can create an
incredible sense of flow. When we
have our sea legs, we can maintain
a peaceful state of mind in the
middle of all life's difficulties. By
simply shifting our relationship to
all that is around us, we are able to
turn misery into ecstasy. Heaven!

IT'S ALL ALRIGHT!

Finding our sea legs is a form of
centering. When we are centered,
we are not affected by externals.
Therefore, it doesn't matter what
table we get, how heavy the
traffic is, how the stock market
rises and falls, and so on.
It's truly all alright!

KEEPING OUR BALANCE

If we leave our center and are
continually reaching out to others
to satisfy some lack within our
selves, we topple forward. If we
constantly withdraw because of
fear, we topple backward in a state
of rigidity. We need to always
come back to center.

CENTERING BRINGS US SERENITY

When we learn how to center ourselves, we are not affected as much by the ebb and flow of life. Our fear diminishes greatly. When things are not going according to plan in our outer life, we are positioned well internally to weather the storm.

NOTHING "OUT THERE" CAN FILL US UP

When we are constantly focused
on externals, we are not centered,
that is, we are not aligned
internally—body, mind and soul.
Without that alignment, we have a
case of Divine Homesickness. We
feel empty and lost, always trying
to find our way Home...always
looking for something
"out there" to fill us up.
And nothing out there can.

AWAKEN THE INTUITION

A centered state is one of immense clarity and focus. As a result, our awareness is heightened and our intuition is sharp. When centered, you can "listen to" and "feel" the environment in and around you. In this heightened state of awareness, you somehow "know" where to go, what to do, what to say, and to whom. Our intuition can always show us the way.

"GOOD" FRIENDS HELP

Develop friendships with positive people rather than "complaint buddies". People who are always complaining are not centered; by definition, they are letting the world around them affect their happiness...and ours, if we allow it! When we choose "centered" friends, we are creating a more stable environment for ourselves.

REACH OUT WITH CONFIDENCE AND LOVE

When entering a room, stand tall as
if you were powerful and loving;
affirm that no matter what reaction
you get, you are a worthwhile
person who has much to give to this
world; focus on what you are going
to give rather what you are going to
get in the way of approval or
acceptance from other people;
radiate your loving energy from your
center to everyone around you.

SPREAD YOUR LOVE AROUND

Don't hold back. Give the gift of
who you are to everyone around
you. Make your essence warm this
world as far as the eye can see.
Visualize those who receive your
powerful spark of life being
nourished by your gift.
Feel the incredible beauty
of just being alive.

EMBRACING

EXQUISITE MOMENTS

When I was a little girl, my father used to tell me that "life is a mass of boredom, interjected with a few exquisite moments." And for many years, I believed him. But not anymore. I wish he were still alive so that I could tell him that he was mistaken…that life can be a mass of exquisite moments interjected with a few moments of boredom!

LIFE IS HUGE!
LIFE IS TO BE
EMBRACED!

OPEN YOUR EYES

As you open your eyes to the wonder around you, you will find that any of the boredom in your life will immediately be replaced by exquisite moments. Your joy, your happiness, your satisfaction and your ability to dance with life depend solely on what you pay attention to. Thankfully, what you pay attention to is entirely up to you!

DON'T TAKE THINGS FOR GRANTED

Taking things for granted is one of the greatest assaults on the quality of our lives. When we take things for granted, we never get to see the magnitude of the gifts that are constantly being placed before us. As a result, we feel only scarcity instead of abundance. The truth is *there is so much to be grateful for that it staggers the imagination!*

MAKE THE ORDINARY EXTRAORDINARY

We need to see things anew.
We need to make the ordinary
in our life extraordinary. When
we do this, things may remain
the same on the outside, but
internally, a gentle revolution
is taking place. Little by little,
we begin to replace the struggl
in our lives with a sense of
abundant flow.

LOOK MINDFULLY

We can embrace the gifts of
magic and excitement in the
most ordinary of events—eating
breakfast, balancing our checkbook,
getting our cars washed, driving to
work, caring for a loved one,
working, brushing our teeth, and
so on. The trick is to learn how
to live in the moment, paying
attention to the wonder of it all.

LOOK DEEPLY

Most of us only skim the
surface when we look at
what life gives to us. This is
why we habitually take
things for granted and miss
the miracle of it all. As we
look deeply, we see that in
everything we do, we have
been handed the Kingdom.
May we always remember this.

SAY "THANK YOU" FOR ALL YOUR GIFTS

The inclusion of the words THANK YOU in our vocabulary sets up an interesting paradox. Each time we say these two powerful words, we are acknowledging a gift we are given. By definition, if we say THANK YOU often enough, any trace of a poverty consciousness disappears; we begin feeling incredibly abundant!

GIVING
FEELS GREAT

Giving is an important part of
embracing our abundance. Make it
a daily ritual to include one pay-
back item on your daily to-do
list—whether it's contributing time
or money to one of your favorite
charities, sending a thank you
note, buying a gift for someone, or
whatever it is for you. No question
about it! Giving feels great!

GIVING COMES FROM THE BEST OF WHO WE ARE

Giving is Higher Self behavior.
As we become a giver, we lose
our temper less, we care
more about the state of the
environment, we don't need as
much as we thought we did,
we are kinder to others.
Giving has many ripple effects
in making ours an incredibly
wonderful world.

DON'T MISS OUT
ON ANOTHER
MOMENT OF
GREATNESS IN
YOUR LIFE. YOUR
WORLD IS RICH.
HARVEST THE
RICHES NOW!

LISTEN TO

THE SILENCE

QUIET
THE MIND

Whatever the method, the
purpose of quieting the mind
is always the same—to step
out of our own way and
touch a Universal oneness
with all things.

LISTEN TO THE WISDOM

In order to fully embrace the riches
in our life, we need to go deep
within our being and listen to the
important messages we hold inside. In
order to do this, we must learn how
to embrace the silence, how to quiet
the endless chatter of the Lower Self,
so that we can hear the wisdom of
the Higher Self.

A QUIET MIND IS A PEACEFUL MIND

One way to quiet the mind is through meditation. In meditation, we watch our thoughts passing by as if they were clouds on a sunny day. We learn that thoughts are just thoughts, and we don't have to get attached to the drama they can bring. In thinking this way, we stop our thoughts from driving us crazy. Peace at last!

WAIT FOR THE ANSWER

When something is deeply troubling you, just sit with it. Don't DO anything. Listen to the wisdom within your being. Eventually you will get the answers you are seeking. In the emptiness, all things fall into place. It is a strange paradox that in emptying the mind, we find exquisite fullness.

SILENCE IS THE MUSIC OF SERENITY

As we turn off the sound and move into silence, the dancing can begin. We finally hear the music of our Soul, and it is this that gives us inner peace. And as we listen to the music of our Soul, we mysteriously and wondrously hear the music of everyone else's as well…and we are at one with the world.

TALK TO THE "CHIEF"

Prayer can bring peace to a struggling mind...even if you don't believe in God! But it has to be the right kind of prayer. Prayers that ask for something set us up for an immense amount of disappointment. Sometimes they are answered and sometimes they're not. It's all up to the Grand Design; it's not up to us. We must learn to trust that it's all happening perfectly!

A PRAYER THAT BRINGS US INNER PEACE

The following prayer never disappoints. It is a prayer of trust and appreciation. Take this prayer into your heart and notice the struggle abating and the peace radiating throughout your being:

"I trust that no matter what
happens in my life, it is for my
highest good. And no matter
what happens in the lives of
those I love, it is for their highest
good. From all things put before
us, we shall become stronger
and more loving people. I am
grateful for all the beauty and
opportunity you put into my
life. And in all that I do,
I shall seek to be a channel
for your love."

PEACE AT LAST!

When we pray regularly, using prayers
of trust and appreciation, the benefits
spill over into all areas of our lives. We
come to realize that the Universal
Light is with us at all times. We need
only to tap into it to find an exquisite
piece of "Heaven" that we can take
into our hearts and radiate out to
everyone whose lives touches ours. In
this place, our fear disappears and is
replaced by an intense sense of love
and caring. Yes, peace at last!

LIGHTEN UP

SMILE...A LOT!

We can begin the process of lightening up and bringing joy into our lives with a simple smile. Smile when you are feeling troubled. Smile as you walk down the street. Smile when you awaken each morning. Smile when you look in that mirror. How does it feel? Lighter? Happier? Oh, yes!

LAUGH A LOT!

Laughter releases tension. Laughter makes life wonderful. Laughter balances the heavy with lightness. Laughter is contagious. Laughter brightens up the world!

MASTER THE BELLY LAUGH!

It's easy to create a smile but much harder to create a laugh. But create it we must! Why? Laughter is very healthy. It changes our internal chemistry from negative to positive. Laughter gives us an internal massage, reaching many organs of the body. Laughter is an amazing exercise. And the good news is that it tightens the belly.

SET YOUR DIAL TO
HAPPINESS! YOU OWE
IT TO YOURSELF TO
LAUGH MORE,
PLAY MORE, AND
FULLY EMBRACE THE
EXPERIENCE
OF LIFE!

ALL IN ITS OWN TIME

ALLOW THE MOMENTS OF CONFUSION

Upset in your life is not a sign that something has gone wrong, only that something is changing. Change usually brings confusion. But one day we "live into" clarity once again, at least for a while. Confusion then clarity, confusion then clarity, confusion then clarity—this seems to be the rhythm of growth.

GROWTH HAS ITS OWN PACE

We live in an instant world where everything has speeded up beyond our grasp. But we are not instant people, and that is where much of the confusion lies. Yes, there are many things that can be done speedily, but when it comes to Spiritual growth, the pace is slow. That's just the way it is.

SPIRITUAL GROWTH IS NEVER-ENDING

Never-ending means that there is always much more to learn; you never "get there." Spiritual growth is not a destination. It is a forever process of expanding and exploring and discovering. Therefore, when you focus on the goal, your attention is misplaced. Pay attention to what you need to learn right here and right now.

WHEN WE THINK NOTHING IS HAPPENING...IT IS

There is always an unseen
world of energy moving and
changing within and around us.
TRUST is the essential
ingredient for feeling peaceful
while these unseen forces
do their work.

WHEN WE ARE IMPATIENT, IT MEANS WE HAVE NO TRUST

Everything happens in its own perfect time. From nature we learn to have patience by simply watching how seeds hidden beneath the earth slowly emerge to create bowers of beauty. We learn the concept of "this too shall pass" by watching storms turn into sunshine. We learn about ups and downs by watching the rhythms, the cycles, the ebb and flow, the harmony and the interplay of all things.

LIFE IS AN EXCITING ADVENTURE

If we have the patience to sit there with the attitude of "Aha! I wonder what this experience is going to teach me" then we can live with a spirit of mystery and adventure rather than with a feeling of fear, helplessness and impatience.

Life IS truly exciting!

CHANGE IS THE ONLY CONSTANT

Ultimately, we learn that there are no shortcuts. The process is the process and there's not much we can do about it. We all want the quick and easy, but when it comes to becoming a Spiritual being, speed doesn't work. We are going for a deep change within our being. This is a lifetime process.

SLOW AND STEADY
WINS THE RACE

In a world of deadlines and stress it is wonderful to know that there is one area in our life where it is better not to rush, and that is the area of Spiritual growth.

TIME IS ON
YOUR SIDE

When you stop thinking that you
have to do it all now, your
impatience dissolves into the sweet
flow that is the natural rhythm of
life. And as you continue your
step-by-step journey, inward and
upward to the best of who we are,
life just gets better and better and
better and better.

NOTHING CAN
STOP YOU NOW!

INNER PEACE IS ABOUT...

releasing, embracing, meditating,
being joyful, being mindful, being
balanced, creating rituals, giving
thanks, slowing down, centering,
knowing that all is well,
transcending the petty, climbing
the ladder to true success, feeling
safe, having patience,
flowing with the Universe.

IT'S ALL
WITHIN YOU

You have the power to create
more and more exquisite moments
in your life. These exquisite
moments come with the creation
of an inner trust...trust in the
process, trust in yourself, and trust
in the Divine Mystery of it all.

YOU DESERVE THE
BEST THAT LIFE HAS
TO OFFER. AND IT'S
REASSURING TO
KNOW THAT YOU
DON'T HAVE TO GO
OUTSIDE YOURSELF
TO FIND THE BEST;
IT LIES WITHIN YOUR
VERY BEING:

The best lies within your Higher
Self, the part of you that sees
everything as a glorious adventure,
the part of you that embraces the
gifts that are placed before you,
the part of you that notices and is
grateful for the miracle of it all,
the part of you that knows that
you are a vibrantly meaningful
part of the Grand Design.

YOU'RE ON THE RIGHT PATH

The most important thing you can do for yourself is to follow the Path that takes you to the best of who you are. Finding the enormous amount of power and love that lies within is the secret to ending the struggle and dancing with life. So COMMIT to this wonderful Journey of self-discovery!

COMMITMENT IS POWERFUL

Commitment creates a radiant energy that activates all sorts of "miracles." I've seen these miracles in my life, and you will see them in yours. Trust me when I tell you that there is NOTHING that can stop you once you make that commitment to create a life of trust, peace, beauty, lightness, abundance, love and joy!

**EMBRACE
THE JOURNEY...**

**EMBRACE
WHO YOU ARE...**

**EMBRACE
ALL THERE IS...**

ABOUT THE AUTHOR

Susan Jeffers, Ph.D. is an
international best-selling author
and speaker. Her many books
include *Feel the Fear And Do It Anyway*
(millions of copies sold), the award
winning *Embracing Uncertainty, Feel the
Fear And Beyond, End the Struggle and
Dance With Life, Opening Our Hearts to
Men, Dare to Connect, Life is Huge* and
The Little Book of Confidence.
She lives with her husband in
Los Angeles, California.

Visit Susan's website at
www.susanjeffers.com